WHEREVER WE MEAN TO BE

Also by Robyn Sarah

Poetry

My Shoes Are Killing Me (2015)
Digressions: Prose Poems, Collage Poems, and Sketches (2012)
Pause for Breath (2009)
A Day's Grace (2003)
Questions About The Stars (1998)
The Touchstone: Poems New and Selected (1992)
Becoming Light (1987)
Anyone Skating On That Middle Ground (1984)
The Space Between Sleep and Waking (1981)
Shadowplay (1978)

Short Stories

Promise of Shelter (1997)
A Nice Gazebo (1992)

Criticism

Little Eurekas: A Decade's Thoughts on Poetry (2007)

Wherever We Mean to Be

Selected Poems 1975–2015

Robyn Sarah

BIBLIOASIS
WINDSOR, ON

Library and Archives Canada Cataloguing in Publication

Sarah, Robyn,
[Poems. Selections]
    Wherever we mean to be : selected poems, 1975-2015
/ Robyn Sarah.

Issued in print and electronic formats.

ISBN 978-1-77196-180-6 (softcover).--ISBN 978-1-77196-181-3 (ebook)

    I. Title.

PS8587.A3765A6 2017   C811'.54   C2017-903643-2
                                           C2017-903644-0

Readied for the press by Daniel Wells
Copy-edited by Emily Donaldson
Typeset by Ellie Hastings
Cover designed by Chris Andrechek

Published with the generous assistance of the Canada Council for the Arts, which last year invested $153 million to bring the arts to Canadians throughout the country, and the financial support of the Government of Canada. Biblioasis also acknowledges the support of the Ontario Arts Council (OAC), an agency of the Government of Ontario, which last year funded 1,709 individual artists and 1,078 organizations in 204 communities across Ontario, for a total of $52.1 million, and the contribution of the Government of Ontario through the Ontario Book Publishing Tax Credit and the Ontario Media Development Corporation.

Poems from *A Day's Grace* were first published by Porcupine's Quill in 2003. Used by permission.

Back cover excerpt from "The World Is Its Own Museum."

Contents

(from *My Shoes Are Killing Me*, 2015)

For Eli Herscovitch

dear friend,
musician *par excellence*, master storyteller,
true believer in poetry, irrepressible spirit,
mensch

Author's Preface

Twenty-five years have passed since I last compiled a selection of my own poems. *The Touchstone: Poems New and Selected* (1992) was reprinted substantially from four earlier titles, all out of print, and has itself been out of print for a decade. The current selection represents the early books (up to and including the twenty-six "New" poems in *The Touchstone*) as well as four titles published since. The selection is again my own, with some qualifications.

I've heard it argued that poets are not necessarily the best judges of their own work and ought not to compile their own Selecteds. I've also heard it argued that a Selected compiled by the poet is of greater interest than one compiled by somebody else, because it identifies the poems most important to the poet. What I think inarguable is that a volume of Selected Poems, regardless of who selected them, can never be sure of pleasing everyone who has some familiarity with the poet's work. Response to poems is so individual. It seems to be a law of Selecteds that the poem one is looking for—whether it be the poem that knocked one's socks off on first encounter, the poem one vaguely remembers and wants to read again, the all-time personal favourite, or the poem one urgently wants to show somebody because it is perfect for the moment or occasion—is not to be found therein.

Still, one tries. In selecting for this volume, I first made a personal long list without looking at my 1992 selection, which then stood as a second take on the early books. I solicited the help of three respected fellow poets with very different voices, all of whom have known my poetry from its beginnings, and asked them to make their own lists, independently of one another and without having seen mine. Finally, I made lists of poems that have been anthologized or broadcast, and poems that have proved favourites at public readings. Comparing lists was instructive, and made me reconsider some of my own choices and exclusions. Thankfully, a core body of poems emerged on which there was some consensus (they are all included), but so did a much larger body of nominees—nearly twice as many as could be accommodated by the book's projected page count.

It was a challenge to settle on the ninety-seven poems I finally selected for this volume. Are they the ones most important to the poet? For the most part, yes—if not the only ones, and if not always for reasons entirely mine (my readers are important to me, too). Would an impartial editor have chosen the same poems? Would I myself choose the same poems if I were doing this five years from now? Moot questions.

For now, I chose these. (And considered calling the book *For Now*.) Without further ado, here they are.

–Robyn Sarah
March, 2017

Broom at Twilight

Some climbs end nowhere. Like the unplanned climb
I took this evening.
                              I'd gone down the beach
some little way, and though the sun was low,
I thought that it would see me round those rocks
to the next cove, with time enough to watch
the tide come in (and maybe make it back
without getting my feet wet.)
                              No such luck—
beyond that stretch, the tide was in already,
and there was nothing to do but climb the cliffs
up to the road, and walk back home that way.

Dark doesn't wait, this time of year. I climbed,
and the sun went down as I went up. Went right on
falling beyond the unseen edge faster
than I could find my holds. (Footholds in clay,
handholds on anchored roots. And all the while
the sky fast darkening out from above.)

                              Near water,
the grey hour's luminous. And by the beach
I should have had no trouble finding my way.
Where I came up, though—something blocked the light.
It was the sameness that surprised me.
                              Broom:

a forest of it. Higher than my head.
And not in clumps, the way it seems to grow
by day—but in a solid wall. An army
bristling with strange intent. The broom I knew
grew in tall waving tufts like uncut hay
to wade through at high noon. This broom stood up
like earth's raised hackles in the failing light —
a massing of ominous spikes against the sky

and stems that wouldn't give way. I couldn't find
the mouse-paths children make to get to the sea—
but had to plunge (broom closing over me)
into a tangible edgeless element,
banking on where I thought the road must be.

Sinkers

If in sudden and several places the ground
you walked on wore thin, or opened up
clear through to the other side—what then?
I can remember when it did: spring rain
left holes in parking lots—holes full of sky
where clouds bloomed and expanded like the milk in tea.
We liked to stand on the edge of them: look down
at what we knew was up, but might as well
exist below as above us (why not?)—and tease ourselves
with fear of falling in. Of stepping
one step too far, right over the edge and
down, down into sky without end. Only, to try
with just one round-toed rubber boot, was to bend
the window back into water: once wavy,
that sky lost its power to pull us in.

Now rain-pools are just things to walk around
or step over. But to keep the ground
from seeming too sure under us, there are eyes
that open up bottomless as those sky-holes
to catch us in our tracks. And we keep dreaming
of a clean fall through to the other side—
unasked-for, with a cushioned landing,
and no charge for the ride.

Fugue

Women are on their way
to the new country. The men watch
from high office windows
while the women go.
They do not get very far
in a day. You can still see them
from high office windows.

Women are on their way
to the new country. They are taking
it all with them: rugs,
pianos, children. Or they are leaving
it all behind them: cats,
plants, children.
They do not get very far in a day.

Some women travel alone
to the new country. Some
with a child, or children.
Some go in pairs or groups
or in pairs with a child
or children. Some in a group with
cats, plants, children.

They do not get very far in a day.
They must stop to bake bread on the road
to the new country, and to share
bread with other women. Children
outgrow their clothes and shed them
for smaller children. The women too
shed clothes, put on each other's

cats, plants, children, and at full moon
no one remembers the way to the new country
where there will be room for everyone and
it will be summer and children will
shed their clothes and the loaves will
rise without yeast and women will have come
so far that no one can see them, even from

high office windows.

Maintenance

Sometimes the best I can do
is homemade soup, or a patch on the knee
of the baby's overalls.
Things you couldn't call poems.
Things that spread in the head,
that swallow
whole afternoons, weigh down the week
till the elastic's gone right out of it—
so gone
it doesn't even snap when it breaks.
And one spent week's
just like the shapeless bag
of another. Monthsful of them,
with new ones rolling in and
filling up with the same junk: toys
under the bed, eggplant slices sweating
on the breadboard, the washing machine
spewing suds into the toilet, socks
drying on the radiator and falling down
behind it where the dust lies furry and
full of itself... The dust!
what I could tell you about
the dust. How it eats things—
pencils, caps from ballpoint pens,
plastic sheep, alphabet blocks.
How it spins cocoons
around them, clumps up and
smothers whatever strays into
its reaches—buttons,
pennies, marbles—and then
how it lifts, all of a piece,

dust-pelts
thick as the best velvet
on the bottom of the mop.
                              Sometimes
the best that I can do
is maintenance: the eaten
replaced by the soon-to-be-eaten, the raw
by the cooked, the spilled-on
by the washed and dried, the ripped
by the mended; empty cartons
heaved down the cellar stairs, the
cans stacked on the ledge, debris
sealed up in monstrous snot-green bags
for the garbage man.

And I'll tell you what
they don't usually tell you: there's no
poetry in it. There's no poetry
in scraping concrete off the high-chair tray
with a bent kitchen knife, or fishing
with broomstick behind the fridge
for a lodged ball. None in the sink
that's always full, concealing its cargo
of crockery under a head
of greasy suds. Maybe you've heard
that there are compensations? That, too's
a myth. It doesn't work that way.
The planes are separate. Even if there are
moments each day that take you by the heart
and shake the dance back into it, that you lost
the beat of, somewhere years behind—even if
in the clear eye of such a moment you catch
a glimpse of the only thing worth looking for—

to call this compensation, is to demean.
The planes are separate. And it's the
other one, the one called maintenance,
I mostly am shouting about.
I mean the day-to-day,
that bogs the mind, voice, hands
with things you couldn't call poems.
I mean the thread that breaks.
The dust between
typewriter keys.

Nocturne

She sits up late, listening
to the wind in leaves that
may be gone tomorrow: one gust
this time of year, and up they fly,
there is no calling them back, and
it will always happen too quickly:
                              Midnight;
in the next room the child
stirs in his crib, cries out
without waking—she thinks of sleep
but sits on, unmoving; a moth
flops in the lampshade, the chairs
cast straight shadows. What
keeps her here at this hour, what—
in the plainness of things, the bare floor,
the broom in the corner, the tea stains
on the frayed tablecloth—sharpens her nerve
to the quiver of a flame-end?
She thinks: Alive.

Down the alley a dog begins barking.
The tree shakes with a knowing
the bones soon share.

Cat's Cradle

When women together sit sipping
cold tea and tugging at the
threads of memory, thoughtfully
pulling at this
or that bit or loop, or slipping
this loop over that finger till
warp and weft of past lives begin
crazily to unwind, when women sit
smoking and talking, the talk
making smoke in the air, when they shake
shreds of tobacco out of a crumpled pack
and keep drinking the same weak tea
from the same broken pot, something clicks
in the springs of the clock
and it's yesterday again,
and the sprung yarn rolls down loose
from the spool of the moon.

When women together sit talking
an afternoon, when they talk
the sun down, talk stars, talk
dawn—they talk up a dust
of sleeping dogs and bones
and they talk a drum for the dust
to dance to, till the dance
drums up a storm; when women
sit drumming fingers on tops
of tables, when the tables turn
into tops that spin and hum
and the bobbin of the moon
keeps spinning its fine yarn down
to catch fingers, when fingers catch
talk in a cat's cradle, and turn
talk into a net to catch the curve
of the storm—then it's talk

against talk, till the tail
of the storm trails into dust
and they talk the dust back down.

Things that matter and don't matter
are caught together, things done and undone,
and the kettle boils dry and over
while they lean closer to peer down
into the murky water where last night's dream
flicks its tail and is gone
(and the reel of the moon keeps cranking
its long line down)—when women together
sit sipping cold tea and sawing on the strings
of memory, it is an old tune.
The rice sticks to the bottom of the pan,
and things get left out in the rain.

At Dawn

At dawn when the lean
young men went loping
homeward from points unknown,
when their streetlamp shadows
on the blue ground
stretched long and small,
scarves
of wondrous colours
flew out behind them,
and their long hands
made fierce talk
in the air.

When the lean young men
went loping sleepward
to basement rooms, sparrows
were trying their voices'
edges against brick. The first
buses chuffed over the hill.
The lean
young men, if they craned
skyward while they fumbled
their keys in cold
barrels, saw how with
each wash of the light
above tortuous rooflines
colour drained
from the moon's face.

How oddly hung
the vestments of
the lean young men,
the outside pockets
weighted
with strange tomes.
Pens bristled in their shirts

and slid
onto the bed
when they bent to kiss
their moon-faced ladies. Other
pens, fat fountain pens
of curious vintage, slept
next to their hearts
and bled black ink
on the inside linings
of their jackets.

At two or three,
in tattered paisley
dressing-gowns
the lean young men
breakfasted on sardines.
Under their eyes
the dark lines
were like war paint
no bath
drawn in a drafty john
could smooth away.
At tables
makeshift and rickety
they scratched
poems in black-bound notebooks
or transcribed
peculiar musicks of a bygone age
for the guitar.
Dusk found the
lean young men
enthroned in clouds
of bluish smoke,

poking with bristle-wires
the stems
of their gummy pipes.

The lean young men
had tongues like fish
and arms
hard as a tree
and bodies warm as furnaces
and though their kisses
tasted
like lemon cough drops
and stale tobacco,
they tossed the hair
from their eyes
with an animal grace
in those days
when they were sought
as seers
and they were loved
like gods

Tides

After nine months
of strangely equal days, then ten
clocked by the press and flood
of milk, her child
eats fruit with his fingers
and scrambles after her, hands pulling her skirt.
Seasons have changed
and she hasn't noticed. One day
she woke up, and it was fall—
another, the snow was melting;
always she fell back
into the close dream where his little face
was sun and moon.
Now, like a young girl, wide-eyed
in the sudden light of outside
she feels it begin
again—like the end
of a sleep she never would have thought
possible, like the waking
of a stopped pulse ticking the world
back into being. Familiar
as an old tune, but this time felt
with a new vibration, the echo
of that huge splash upon whose ripples
she has been riding—it comes again:
the downward tug of the blood
at full moon,
amazing as the sound
of the first rain.

An Early Start in Midwinter

The freeze is on. At six a scattering
of sickly lights shine pale in kitchen windows.
Thermostats are adjusted. Furnaces
blast on with a whoosh. And day
rumbles up out of cellars to the tune
of bacon spitting in a greasy pan.

Scrape your nail along the window-pane,
shave off a curl of frost. Or press your thumb
against the film of white to melt an eye
onto the fire escape. All night
pipes ticked and grumbled like sore bones.
The tap runs rust over your chapped hands.

Sweep last night's toast-crumbs off the tablecloth.
Puncture your egg-yolk with a prong of fork
so gold runs over the white. And sip
your coffee scalding hot. The radio
says you are out ahead, with time to spare.
Your clothes are waiting folded on the chair.

This is your hour to dream. The radio
says that the freeze is on, and may go on
weeks without end. You barely hear the warning.
Dreaming of orange and red, the hot-tongued flowers
that winter sunrise mimics, you go out
in the dark. And zero floats you into morning.

The Cyclist Recovers His Cadence

i

When the front wheel
glances off something hard
you are thrown over
the handlebars and slap
pavement with a crunch
of bone. In that instant
a hole opens under you
and it goes clear down
to the howling centre.
You wake there. It is a while
before you become aware
of an odd jazz playing
and longer still before your feet
begin to move to it.

Nothing can be the same
from here. The smells
that blow in open windows
of an evening: honeysuckle
and fried potatoes, a mix
sure to confuse   even your childhood
has an unfamiliar patina
when you lie awake
remembering it. Summer
is upon you, heat, the sticky
surfaces of things. You long
strangely for thunder, but when it comes
it's not the ticket.
The old box has cracks in it.
The old box
                    The crank
on the ice cream bucket

slips a gear. Children
gather, they jump like flies
around a lamp, bouncing
off each other. One, the biggest,
thwacks the ice in a burlap sack
against the concrete step.
Your bad arm gives out
as the mixture stiffens.
Switch to the left. The crew
runs home for spoons.

Later, cutting the grass
to work off steam, coming out
in the dark to dust the beets
with rotenone, unkinking
the garden hose, nothing
means what you thought it did,
your mother's letter invoking God ·
notwithstanding, you draw a blank
in the higher uncertainties.
Enough if in the after-dinner hours
neighbours gather on the stoops
till long past dark, enough
that your son dances barefoot
on the pavement, blowing
harmonica tunes to the night street.

ii

Summer
sprints fallward, but all else
is sluggish, still. The clothes
on the line hang damp for days.
Noon vibrates
like sheet metal
Cicadas drill
        Fruit flies
cluster to kiss the broken skins
of blue plums rotting on the window sill.

The body's knit itself.
You celebrate your thirtieth
on the muggiest day of summer.
Somewhere a bicycle wheel
spins on, up-ended,
and though you know the trick
that's kept it going, its oilsmooth
tickticktick still calibrates
the space between sleep and waking.
The spokes flash in the sun
and seem
to reverse direction. When it stops—

iii

becomes-still.
One piano tone struck in an empty room.
Pain's stab
ebbing. The candle
drowning in its own wax.

Spun to nothing.
No end, but
continuum.
Beginnings flow out of this.

Soft-pedalling the *da capo*,
the soul's progress
diminuendo

iv

At the bottom of the key
fullness hangs
on a fingertip. See,
a moon-sliver; the blanched
rim of the nail.
Blood presses
against it. At rest
like this, sunk
in a tuned stillness
the hand becomes
capable of motion.

You are working your way back
towards a more placid grammar.
Your son points at the moon
and laughs. You carry him to bed.

If the little fox gets his tail in the water,
what could further?

V

Delicately between her teeth
your grandmother cracks
blanched almonds into
their clean, separate halves.
Sunset from a folding chair.
Your mother on the screened porch
calls a warning. A clear
soprano
           You are stepping over
the wire fence, you are putting
one foot down
into the fields. Ping!
a grasshopper flies up
like a sprung paper clip.
Ping   Ping   A tawny sea
closes back over them. One
step more, and a knot
in the grass unfoots you,
flings you on your face
in prickles. You cry
and they run to lift you back
into the garden. A bird
pipes in the thicket. Soon
they will carry you to bed.

The moon comes out
like a chip of blanched almond.

vi

Take it again from the beginning,
run the reel backward
to the point of collision,
repeat the vault
in slow motion.
There was your chance,
there is what
you must all along have been
waiting for, it will
happen again, you have been
primed. While the wheel spins
the spokes wink out their music.
Take your boy's hands
and dance. Complete
these revolutions
till the neat
rebuff, the unseating,
the somersault into
another country.

End to End

Feet, how did you get so far away?
I watch you from the other end
of the bathtub—the pair of you,
animals, carrying me around
thirty years now, like good
beasts of burden. Time was
when I saddled you first in
patent leather, you dazzled
my eyes, showing me my
face, twinned, in black lacquer.
Then you were nearer; near
the years I rode you hard
in scuffed Oxfords, rode you
bare, summers, over
beach-shingle, road-gravel,
buried you in lakemuck
aired you out the car window
trailed you in silken water
over the side of the boat.
Hitched around chairlegs
you tapped impatience, chafed
at the rungs till they popped
their sockets. Time came
I rode you bare again
in protest: you slapped hot
asphalt, wet sidewalks, cool tiled
floors in public buildings, your
soles grew another skin, horny
black hide I soaked off
at the end of the season.

Look at you now,
demure there, perched
on white porcelain—odd fish
half out of water, old mates—when did this
length come between us, this

body of a woman
which has already produced
out of itself other bodies?
You are still the same old
feet, preferring to go shoeless,
jumpy under tables, one of you
thumping the bed like a cat's tail
nights when sleep takes its
sweet time coming—but you are a
distance off now, beyond where I
can take you in my hands
without torsions. Feet, I
salute you here, from my own
end of the tub. I shall soak on
till the pads of your toes
wrinkle. (At my bidding
the ten of them flex towards me,
bowing.)

In Winter Rooms

In winter rooms, the sad grey light settles on breakfast remains. On the knife that rests against the saucer, and on the crumbs in the glass dish. On the crumbs in the butter. And the piece of burnt toast with two bites out of it, left to get cold on the tablecloth.

It is the same light, whether morning or afternoon. It picks out the new cracks in the plaster, the streaks on the ceiling; it catches the tremble of a long feather of soot which hangs by an invisible hair from a joint in the chimney-pipe. The sad grey light comes leaking through dirty panes; it circles the room like a ghost and does not chase the shadows. Only the round belly of the brown teapot, glazed and shining, catches a gleam of it and flashes it back like a drop of water.

Outside, snow piles on the balcony rail and on the sill. A rag flaps in the balcony tree; it has been flapping there for a hundred days. Torn plastic billows out from the shed windows. Sometimes there are sparrows; they don't sing though. The leaves of the house-plants dry and curl up; now and then one falls off and crumbles into dust. Wind comes down the chimney and blows the smell of oilsoot into the house.

In a corner of the kitchen, the old woman rocks and rocks in the rocking chair. The young woman is making bread, pounding the dough on a wooden board. A dust of flour is on the air. She pounds and thumps the dough until her strong knuckles ache, and then she oils a bowl in which to let it rise.

The child plays on the floor. She has begged a piece of dough for her own, and has rolled it between her palms until it is grey and without resilience. Now its creases persist; it will no longer roll back into smoothness. The child tires of it; she asks to take down the green vase from the shelf, the vase with the chipped rim. She empties it of its contents: stray buttons, pennies, hairpins, a single earring, pencil-stubs, and keys that don't belong to anything. These she picks up one by one and examines intently, dropping some back into the vase and making a little pile of others beside her right knee.

THE rockers wear away the pattern on the linoleum.
The child discovers her face in a spoon, upside down.
The young woman punches the dough down and forms
it into loaves.

THE rockers fret and fret against the floor; they wear the
pattern off the linoleum.
The teapot like a dark bubble reflects the sad grey square
of window.
The child bites into an orange and peels it. The essence
stings the air. She offers a wedge to the young woman,
who takes it and eats. She offers a wedge to the old
woman, who does the same.

ON the shelf above the stove, the loaves rise.

The umbrellas have shut

The umbrellas have shut.
They have folded
old lovers into them.
The old rainy nights
are fled, with their little
lights winking between wet
leaves, the pearled panes
under the lamps, the stairs
creaking, slick-
wet and pasted with catkins.
And the old rooms, the rooms
ornate and empty, echoing
and smelling of fresh paint—
almost
we do not remember—
and the cats on windowsills,
the hamburger smells, the guitars.

When it rains now
it is colder, we do not run
pressed close together for the nearest
café, fall's loosed leaves lie
ungathered at the curb.
The umbrellas have collapsed their domes.
They have pulled in their petals
softly dripping, have sucked
a decade into their ribs
like a sigh. Only now and then
when wind
comes charged with the old changes,
or a hat thrown on a shelf spills down
a landslide of letters
do we regret
the tall sticks
furled
in hall closets.

The Search

The search begins again, just
when you thought you'd arrived, or
anyway ceased to stumble, grown
content with randomness, with wandering
as an end in itself. You like the
woods, even at night, the fields
mornings or afternoons, you've beaten a
path in the long grass from the back door
to your spot overlooking the valley.
Little enough you care if your foot slips
into the odd bog, take that as a cue
to stretch out in clover, chewing
on a grass-blade while your socks
dry out in the sun. What else
could you say you wanted? Even so
you feel it come on, sometimes, like the
mournful magic of those augmented
triads the frogs raise, their long, slow
trills bubbling up in the moonlight.

It has never helped to think you knew
what you were looking for, and now
you know you don't: that maybe when all's said
it isn't you who look, but someone
or something out there, in the watchful
dark, that has followed you to this pass
and waits only for you to walk
unwitting into its arms. Night itself
is full of surprises, a stray firefly
winks in the windbent upper branches
of the pine grove, clouds
cocoon the moon
and you stand still, thinking it's
right beside you—there—or there—
though your hands close only
on air, and once again the frogs sing
something you've never heard before.

Sounding an Old Chord in October

The streetlamp directly opposite
is out, an unaccustomed dark
pools this side of the street.
In the garden the dried bean-pods
rasp on their woody vines,
leave nothing to look forward to
but snow. Still, expectation
stirs, a dog with ears cocked
for familiar footsteps, lights
in strange windows are taking on
a peculiar intimacy
                    It's the old story,
the thing we'd almost forgotten, last year's
chestnut, bone-smooth to cold fingers
fishing a linty pocket for a fare
(though the rates have gone up again
since the coat was hung away, and any
loose change is purely fortuitous)

A pebble
ricochets off the bus-stop
with the kind of ping metal only makes
when cold, like the twang
of a piano-string that slips
in the dead of night
                  so expecting
the unexpected becomes a way of saying
yes again, this is the thing
we refuse to go on without,
the delicate engineering of a life
to allow for a coincidence of paths,
take it from there

For no other reason
we stare at a little piece of street
between buildings, as if we could will
the arrival of someone unlikely to pass there,
spontaneous, nonchalant,
with neither wine nor flowers,
just a dark figure jaunting along
in no sort of hurry
and visible only for seconds
between parked cars.

A Meditation Between Claims

You want to close your hand
on something perfect, you want to say
Aha. Everything moves towards this,
or seems to move, you measure it
in the inches you must let down
on the children's overalls,
tearing the pages off the wall
each month; a friend phones
with news that another friend
has taken Tibetan vows, meanwhile the
kitchen is filling up with the smell
of burnt rice, you remind yourself
to buy postage stamps tomorrow

The mover
and the thing moved, are they two
or one; if two, is the thing moved
within or without, questions
you do not often bother yourself with
though you should; the corner store
is closed for the high holy days,
and though the air has a smell
not far from snow, your reluctance
to strip the garden is understandable

Laundry is piling up
in the back room, Mondays and Thursdays
the trash must be carried out
or it accumulates, each day
things get moved about and
put back in their places
and you accept this, the shape
that it gives a life, though the need
to make room supersedes other needs

If, bidding your guest goodbye,
you stand too long at the open door,
house-heat escapes, and the oil bill
will be higher next month, the toll
continues, wrapping the green tomatoes
in news of the latest assassination.
The mover
and the thing moved, it all
comes down to this: one wants
to sit in the sun like a stone,
one wants to move the stone; which
is better

Intermezzo in a Minor Key

Cats walk the slats
of a city afternoon
in winter: and that twist
of fire-escape that skirts
your window giving
on a brick well. One imagines
how it fills up slowly
with snow—and your world
of jazz and old photographs
wavers in shifts of light
filtered down between buildings,
while smells of frying gather
on the landing, and the clumps of dust
under the peeling rads blow about a bit
in the draft from the door...

One thinking of you this way,
at a sharp remove, desires
no more than the evocation
of a time long past or yet to come:
"No one phoned while you were out"
or the concierge knocks to collect the rent
and the scene has its welcome shadings,
yearning held in abeyance, blurred over,
like hearing the news through the wall
on somebody else's radio.

Refilling the Spirit Lamp

For a while desire is fuel.
And the distance gained
always is illusory.
There's a luminescence young
leaves can't hold very long
in their greening, or the air
in early spring, when it is cool
and frangible, that is
something like what we thought
had been promised:

how a cup, a lamp, a chair
are so much more than that,
or the scarf you left behind, a
handful of loose change on the bureau.
Someone saw a common thread there
and named it, but he didn't know
how close a brush it had been.

What burns now
is something else, something we hope
could be more dependable, riding out
a run of bad weather, how these
evenings find us back in our rooms
over paper, our lamps tuned low,
and an ear for the finest of nuances
bent to that tuning

Paperweight

i

She accustoms herself
to his silences. They seem
rich, like soup; slow, like
soup. They heat up slowly
and thicken. There is no
telling what is in them.

ii

He moves the furniture around.
He reads cookbooks.

iii

She dreams she has broken
his little hammer, the one he uses
to play tunes on the base of his lamp.
(He has no little hammer.)

iv

He picks up the papers
wind has scattered from her desk.
He gives her an old candle
for a paperweight. (In a note
he tells her to use it
as a paperweight.)

v

When he isn't there
she notices things
that trouble her. When he
is there, she notices
the same things.

vi

He wakes up at night
and thinks he hears pages
turning.

Pardon Me

The rip in the sleeve of your jacket, and the fact that I do not have to mend it, are conjoined in a way that you do not understand. You do not understand because you do not know that there is a rip in the sleeve of your jacket, and I do not have to tell you because I do not have to mend it. This is not the same as to say that I do not have to mend it because I am not going to tell you it is there, which would be a stall at best. Maybe you do know that there is a rip in the sleeve of your jacket, but if you do, you would not mention it to me because you know that I do not have to mend it.

Because I do not have to mend it, and because you do not seem to mind wearing it with a rip in the sleeve, your jacket is becoming a kind of statement to me of all that does and does not exist between us, including what you do not know about what I feel about your wearing it with a rip in the sleeve. There is also what I do not know about what you would feel if you knew my feelings. I am not going to tell you what I feel about your wearing your jacket with a rip in the sleeve because if you do not know there is a rip in the sleeve, you might be less than pleased to find out—especially as I do not have to mend it. Moreover, I might be less than pleased to find out that had you known there was a rip in the sleeve, you would not have been wearing your jacket.

To avoid mutual disappointment, I do not touch on this matter which, even assuming you do know there is a rip in the sleeve, you are doubtless not thinking about. Besides, there is always the danger that my mention of a rip in the sleeve might be interpreted as an offer to mend it, a desire to mend it, or a wish to see it mended. That is not what I meant at all; that is not it, at all.

Water on the Chair

Things we want
in the dark—
because—

the lop-eared lamb
wedged between wall
and frame, him,

smelling of mildew
and old pee—
called for

a hundred times
without emphasis,
with a blind

insistence, need
to have him
dragged up

dusty and begrudged
from that place
we can't see—

Things we call for
in the dark,
uncalled-for—

the full glass
near to hand
sipped from   once only

along whose sides
by morning
small pearls have formed—.

On My Son's Birthday

Already the beans have begun their wild climb,
twining tough runners round and round each string
we anchored to the porch above our own.
Only a month ago, you helped me press
the seeds we popped from dry brown pods last fall
into the holes you poked with your small fingers.

Today you wake me, holding up five fingers
to mark your years, triumphant, as you climb
beside me into bed, but not to fall
asleep again. Later you know we'll string
balloons, wrap favours. Eager, your cold feet press
for warmth, toes curled tight, against my own.

This is our day, this day you call your own.
Five years ago today, I counted fingers,
touched perfect limbs, and felt your small mouth press
against my nipple. After our breathless climb
we lay together, linked by a tough string
cut cleanly to allow your perfect fall.

First-fruit; conceived, not like our beans, in fall,
popped from the pod in summer. This has its own
logic, I think; I touch it like a string
and feel it resonate beneath my fingers.
The months are like the scale's twelve tones we climb
yearly, as toward this fundament they press.

Born at the solstice. Born when light's clean press
toward summer scales its height and points to fall,
but when the vines have just begun their climb
into the light to rhythms of their own
with leaves uncurling like a baby's fingers.
This is the day the arrow left the string.

Lying beside me now, taut as that string
with all the day's solemnity, you press
your hand against my hand to measure fingers,
show me scraped knuckles from a recent fall,
tell me you'd like a scooter of your own.
Outside, the sun begins its perfect climb.

My sprout, my vine, my own, God guard your climb
and string you toward your flowering. As my years press
toward fall, I count my blessings on your fingers.

Black Walnut

We found those funny green balls in the grass,
perfumy as unripe oranges, but hard,
and bleeding rank iodine when cut open,
leaving their stain deep in the palms' creases.
The stone inside was hard to hack away
from the raw flesh of the stubborn fruit.

Now, heading into winter, one fruit
of the several we picked up that day in the grass
sits on the sill, where I put it away
to see if it would ripen. Blackish, rock hard
though light as pumice, it has dried in ridged creases.
It would take a hammer to break this open.

But who would ever think of breaking it open?
It seems an artifact now, not a fruit.
Its history is sealed into these creases
as ice preserves the lay of the tangled grass.
I have no use for this thing; why is it hard
to decide the time has come to throw it away?

Maybe because the scent has not gone away,
and the faint spice of it has power to open
thought-ways to other things grown soft or hard
with age or their own failure to yield fruit
(though they persist, unkillable as the grass
that, flattened, springs back up from its own creases.)

I think how ice moves over the earth, and creases
the face of it, or grinds the edges away,
leaving a smooth bed for the blanketing grass.
I think how, in the rock, deep fissures open
and endure to become valleys, lush with fruit—
and then, how rotting trees have turned stone hard.

And I think of the passion to preserve, the hard
clear light that loves to register the creases
in a face, or a cloth with an arrangement of fruit:
as if recording these could hold away
the shadow of that chasm we know must open
soon at our feet, in the supple familiar grass.

Hard as its nut, this mummy of a fruit
creases the brow. The mind drifts far away,
open to every current in the grass.

Suckers for Truth

How much longer do you suppose
we can get away with it, edging
a little closer to the fire, sitting up
long past midnight, stubborn holdouts
in the unseasonable cold? The effects
of too much wine, of wine at the wrong time
have begun to take their toll, dredging up moments
that had gone unnoticed, but return now
to trouble us, like a funny noise
in the engine, that we register gradually
but manage to avoid talking about for miles

The landscape falls away
on either side of us, some of the trees
already turning, far ahead a darkening
as yet more felt than seen, seeming to indicate
we're heading into a storm front
and we don't care, do we, switching the radio
to another station, watching the signs
for a roadside diner, somewhere to unzip
and grab a sandwich, coffees to take out,
while we congratulate ourselves
for making good time

It's not as though we aren't aware
of the pitfalls, but that we know
procrastination is our best defence,
so far we have not committed ourselves
and it shows, there's that comfortable rubble
on the seats and floor we'd have to clear away
to get down to business, oddly festive
and a bit risqué, till now it has seemed
easiest to tack strips of old carpeting
over the cracks, when the thing falls apart
we're hoping it will do it all at once

A camp stool, a tin pot, and an old
umbrella, stage props for a stay
against confusion, we find ways
to laugh at the rain, and in it,
and to accommodate our guests, so much
depends upon the things glimpsed
in the rear-view mirror, wheelbarrows
and such, it seems that with luck
a kind of courtship happens between the lines
and it's this we're after: without the risk
what would be possible?

Little Prelude

Triggered by wind, the twinned
and single wings copter
off maples. Wind
rasps their dry webbing
against pavement, where children,
playing, alone, scoop
handfuls to husk
down to the sappy bean.

Oh summer's big quilted winds
bolstering scent! the chestnut's
gleaming pyramids, catalpa
shaking its frilly bells down
to grass. Green
barely remembered, under
cloud cover, green lit
from within, June green, how it

jumps our eyes, moments
before rain, when the length
of the emptying street, heavy
windows gibber shut
in their wooden frames.

Walking a Dog in the Rain

–If the shoe fits, wear it.

These lessons in patience
weren't asked for. Among
so much else, I'm learning
to recognize them for the gift
they probably are. Like
the rest of it: the varied shades
of brick darkened by rain, odours
of back sheds, mildewed
and dark with promise, bent
objects reaching odd lengths out
from heaps of rotting board
                              It's true
that I've wanted more, again, balanced
against so much I thought I'd
given up on, leaning
on the porch rail, evenings, dreaming my
scrap of yard—what
will grow here? what can grow?
the question like a shy palm
turned up to catch the rain, is this
how it begins, will it be
different this time?

The waiting
obliterates itself, has come to be
a formal exercise, diminishing
in tension, almost a dance,
though months elapse
between gestures and it doesn't matter
in the way that it used to

I like a white wall,
a good lamp, shadows
of leaves, I can live with these
a long time, even

without music, the right pictures
will show up, one at a time, when you're
not looking for them, all the
small touches you've come to expect
are best done without at first,
giving you time
to grow neutral, pure, to shed
the crust of what was

You play back the tape
of nothing happening in your house
and it's nice, it's
just like being there:
                              moments
that can still make me smile

Tracing
and retracing of steps, the paths
now familiar, every pause,
every turn, alleys, vacant lots,
the brickpiles and back fences
with gaps one can navigate, the lamp posts
one lingers under at predictable hours

And again the urge to say
come home now, come in
out of the rain, this is the
hardest lesson, the final one, not
to say it, leave the way clear
for you to recognize what's yours
and claim it
                         a gentle city, generous
in its leaves, the porch lights
burn late there, the double doors

stand open, even now, letting in
fragrance of linden, flowers
litter the stoop where rain drips
from the eaves, wind blows through the
empty rooms, finally
this will always
be enough

The Aging Woman with Braids

And of the balancing acts
of squirrels, of cats, I say
they do recover themselves;

And of the man who walked
a crooked mile, I say
he will remember it;

And of the wet letter, peeled
from rainy pavement, I say
best not read that...

Look! how Love is spawned
in the air, between the white hands
of Pierrot; how it floats there, thin and
inviolate, a bubble, reflecting
the tenderness of his smile—

I am taking five umbrella steps
in my Chinese cloth shoes.
Mother, may I?

Here on Earth

The child is learning the laws of perspective;
with his thumb, he can cover his father's face,
with his palm, he blots whole buildings.
At the right distance, the keyhole—imagine it—
can contain the landlady, fat as she is;
so it would not surprise him if the odd camel
slipped through the eye of a needle.

Heaven is full of rich men,
but the poor, the poor,
(subject to the laws
of perspective, and
other laws)—the poor
are here on earth
for a long time.

Zero Holding

I grow to like the bare
trees and the snow, the bones and fur
of winter. Even the greyness
of the nunneries, they are so grey,
walled all around with grey stones—
and the snow piled up on ledges
of wall and sill, those grey
planes for holding snow: this is how
it will be, months now, all so still,
sunk in itself, only the cold alive,
vibrant, like a wire—and all the
busy chimneys—their ghost-breath,
a rumour of lives warmed within,
rising, rising, and blowing away.

September

It is the
end of summer, in fields
along the canal the smell
of white clover is strong.
The green
cigars of catalpa point down
through clusters of heart-
shaped leaf, they are
raw still, spear-like
and tough to break, the
red froth of the sumacs
wafts a fruit scent.
Finally, what have I to say
to you—walking alone here
among tall and drying weeds,
goldenrod, white sprays
of aster, the shocking blue
of chicory, that makes one see
all else in the light
of that blue? A shimmer
of insect sound is all
around me; grasshoppers
fly at my footsteps, pell-mell
into the roadside grass, I'm trying
to savour the day's gifts, each
for what it is, but thinking
how soon this ends: the clocks
of the maples already tuned
to fall—
        And there's less and less call
to imagine you, living out
your day on the other side
of the river: those streets
where pavement still absorbs
the sun's late heat all afternoon

and gives it back at evening, you're
walking there now, your shoes
don't make a sound, you've loosened
your tie and your jacket's
over your arm, above you glass
sidings catch the sunset light
and flash it down, suffusing your path
in pink, while higher still
on the hillside at the city's
heart, visible in the clefts
between buildings, show those first hints
of the colours we are supposed to find
so beautiful.

Detour

An unexpected turn, and the bus leaves you by a corner you've not seen before—just a bit of city, neat flats above small store fronts, small front yards, here by the corner post a bushel basket planted with zinnias, there a locust tree, blowing against brick, the leaves untidy with autumn. Rain in the air. At your back a corner grocer's; with each swing of the door, whiffs of ripe fruit, of scented soap and onions. Look, across the street an old barber-shop, the striped pole revolving, and the barber moody, hands in pockets, gazing out through plate glass—motionless as the empty chairs behind him.

Sparrows, loud in a hedge. The leaves showing their under-sides. You're not sure what street you're on, but you have your transfer, and what else is needed? This is the day's sole surprise, to find yourself for a short spell in this spot you'll likely not see again, though you pass close to it daily. A place of no importance in the frame of what you call your life. You hope the bus will come before the rain does, you like the look of the lights now, in the shop windows. That's as far as you want to think it, holding your ground here for the time required, taking at face value this place that counts for today only. The place where you count to ten and take the blindfold off. Where you stand and wait, on faith, for your next connection.

Interim

You're on a scaffold, I'm
down below, and you want
to talk yet—as though
talk, on such a slant, meant
anything; you, teetering there
in your high place, without
a rope, and I in a hole
where I can't see your face?
It's a joke, love. Let's wait
till there's at least a hope
of seeing eye to eye—what?
—talk about talking straight.

I'll stay here and make patterns in the gravel.
(Or, call down, and I'll hand you up your level.)

Scratch

The tinder words, where are they,
the ones that
jump-start the heart—

> like mirrors at the bends
> of tunnels, that withhold
> your face, but give you
> what is to come;

> like the voice at the end
> of the tunnel, that says
> 'Terminus', almost
> tenderly—

Little twigs that snap
like gunshot as they
consume themselves, little
dry twigs,

little sparks, little pops, little bursts
at the smoky heart of where it
begins again, o,

tender and sunny love! what, are you gone
so far away?

Come home to me now, my
brightness. Make a small glow.
Make it to move
the heart, that has sat down
in the road

and waits for something
to turn it over...

> The roomy heart,
> willing to be surprised.

To Fill a Life

To fill a life as fitful sky fills windows, or a painter, canvas, to fill it wilfully, to make large movements within a frame, I think is to be desired—the frame, too, not to contain, but to provoke such movement. No mirror will show you the lines worry pushes your face into, for in the looking, curiosity makes other lines. I want to move far enough away to see you whole, as a child will in a loop that he makes of finger and thumb. *Look how small I can make you, Mummy.*

So the unmade beds of children. So the hats, scarves, mitts, thrown pell-mell over the radiator, so the smell of damp wool filling the hall as the heat rises. On the counter, the jagged shells of breakfast eggs, a crust of stuck whites like brown lace in the cast iron skillet still warm on the burner. So the towels on the bathroom floor, the steamed mirror, stray hairs in the tub and a blue worm of dried toothpaste on the edge of the sink. The tap dripping, humid air smelling of shampoo. The face of a life in motion. The pegs on the rack by the door, on which are slung umbrellas, shawls, soft bags of cloth and leather, the straps wound round each other.

To delight in the weathered, more than in polished planes, to prefer the visible repair to the thing re-done, I think is to respect tenancy, its wear and tear, its fixed term. For each grey hair he pulls from her head, she gives her youngest son a penny, until there are so many, he makes a bankrupt of her, no more, she throws up her hands, laughing. Decades later, when she sells the old house, he comes at night and removes from its hinges the door to the back shed, into whose reluctant grain he and his brothers gouged their names and a date, in boyhood. He puts it on his car, he drives it home and stores it under his stairs. Three names on an unhinged door, the first, of a man dead these twenty-two years. All winter, snow blows into the old shed.

To fill a life. To fill one's own shoes, and walk in them till the plies of the soles begin to separate, till the heels are rubbed away, till the toes turn up and the lettering inside has all flaked off. As fitful sky. To go with the drift of things, shifts of the light and weather. Snow blows into the tracks my skis made this morning: erase all that. I am walking on the face of winter. It's like magic, it's like walking on water, it *is* walking on water. Are you listening? I know a man who photographs the bumps on faces, the tiny lines, who celebrates them with his sharpest focus. I know a man who broke his hammer trying to open a window. Each winter new cracks open in the chimney wall, air currents trace fresh strata of soot across the ceiling.

A pulling against the grain. Amoebas of light in the undulation of gauze curtains, the cross and mesh of lines. Water's resistance as the oars reverse direction. Walking upwind. Syncopation, in music, or certain kinds of dissonance. Cloth cut on the bias, hair combed up from the nape. Velvet, rubbed the wrong way with a finger. Or finger and thumb, cleansed to an edge, testing each other's raised grain. Feeling the lines that frame us, whorl and loop, for life, beyond confusion.

I want to move far enough away to see you whole, I want a lens to contain you, even upside down, as a handful of cast type contains its own impression. As winter contains spring, or the residue of snow, the shape of those things it melted around. The broken tricycle, the rusted spade. It is spring, the season for construction; no backward look in the way that old house is gutted for renovation. I watch from across the street, chunks of my life knocked out like bad teeth, the plaster-dust drifting down like a chalky pall over the gardens. Erase all that. Are you listening?

The face of a life in motion. The sound of pianos out of open windows; radios playing to empty kitchens. On the cold sidewalk, a ring of footsteps: that sound nearly forgotten. Clotheslines shrilling on rusty pulleys; the squeak of baby-carriage wheels. Or close your eyes and it's June, pages torn from a child's copy-book are blowing down the street. In the park, by the stone pond, a line of figures in loose clothing practice Tai Chi, their movements sweeping, rhythmical, echoing each other like the arches of the pavilion behind them, reflected in the water. It's early morning. The movements are large, are generous, they flow, and the clothing too as it fills with wind, flapping against the bodies held there in marvellous postures against the light.

Woman on a Bus

The hat that is out
of the ordinary, the off-beat
hat, lends to the face
that is ordinary, an odd
off-beat grace. (It's all in how
she carries herself, that she
carries it off.)

Sometimes a man

Sometimes a man who has missed his bus
still runs after it a little way.
You can see his shoulders first
subside, defeated, but he doesn't slow;
his head knows that it's too late,
but his feet have to go on a bit
doing what they were doing... so.
That's how it is, with feet.

Once, Desire

Once, desire was a soft roaring
between us, like white water,
and we adjusted our voices
to be heard above it
till it seemed to us
that we whispered: as any sound,
heard long enough, becomes silence.

I would like to go back to that time,
when the power was still outside of us
and we were as if asleep, cocooned
in the white rush of it. Unharmed
and unarmed. When we were a
dream of wings. Before this
perilous flying.

Equinox

All the gold has drained
from the light; and these leaves,
littering the grass, caught
in its tangles, where
did they come from?

There was a black horse, one evening,
across a fence, who followed us
a length of the road—

I must have been asleep
all summer.

Passages

All day long, upstairs,
a new mother coos to her baby girl,
and the floorboards creak, creak
under her rocking-chair.

And footsteps go back and forth,
back and forth, in the dead of night,
and yellow light from her kitchen window
suddenly floods the snow.

Coo, coo; motherhood has turned her
into a bird. Silently I tell her: I, too,
once woke in the night with hardened breasts,
and soaked the front of my flannel gown with milk.

Now my daughter stands splay-legged at the mirror
braiding her hair against night-time tangles,
and already her nipples have begun to stand out,
and she crosses her arms over them, shyly.

And upstairs, you read books about infant growth,
with pages of gleaming photographs—
and downstairs, I read books about divorce,
with no photographs at all.

And all day long, snow blows in small showers
from the tree whose branches brush your window.
Bursts of bright powder, glittery in the sun
fall past my window.

Journey

In this house, the furnace and the furnace-pump
make a rumble that shivers the panes
and rattles the rads, till the whole room
throbs like an oiltruck, idling.

And when they shut off: what silence!
In the window, hung by a thread,
a teardrop prism emits a purple spark.
Beneath it, a crocheted snowflake

revolves slowly, seeming to melt into air
at ninety degrees, and then to reappear.
Only a little sun
ever gets in. It's here now—

Then the heat starts up again. Slowly
the rumble picks up a rhythm, something like
the rackety rocking of a train. I close my eyes
and let it carry me...

I will remember this house
for its thundering winters, for the
huge distances they
carried me.

Trial Footage: The Farm

It begins with a man standing alone in the middle of his field, looking at nothing;

It begins with the standing bones of a dead elm, standing elm bones;

With a child on a fence, looking up at clouds moving past the dead elm, and feeling how the tree is slowly falling...

Or with a child lying in the grass, looking up at clouds moving past the barn roof, and feeling how the barn is slowly falling...

Or with the same child, thinking that he is feeling the earth turn.

It begins with a man standing alone in the middle of his barn, looking at nothing;

It begins with a car taking a curve on a dirt road and sliding off the shoulder into the ditch, slow motion, and coming to rest at a sharp angle against a wall of brush,

And in the silence a child in the back seat cries out, "I'm scared—we're going to die!" though the car has already stopped moving.

It begins with a man far down in the lower pasture, his blue shirt glimpsed between trees,

Or with a woman's call to supper, moments before sunset, answered by silence and a rush of wind.

It begins with the child finding an empty bullet case in the dust by the side of the road, and slipping it into his pocket,

Or finding a dead mole by the side of the road, and stroking its velvet fur, and marvelling at its human hands, and digging a hole to bury it beside the barn.

It begins with a man standing alone on a plowed field, looking at nothing,

And it begins to rain on his bare neck, on the slope of his shoulders,

And it begins to wet the lightened hairs on his strong arms hanging loose at his sides,

And it rains down harder on his head, that he lowers against the rain,

It rains on his unruly head.

Shell

I have your hat
in my hands; hat
that holds your head,
what does it know?
And were I to halloo
down into it, to yell
Hey! who lives here?
what could it tell me
of the head it holds?
That old cold head
that won't disclose
its holdings... Love,
I have your hat; keep
what I say under it,
along with what
you don't. (Hat
that holds your head
I would hold
in my hands
instead.)

A Mystery

Around the side of Bob
Jones' barn the children find
the dead calf, frozen
among dry weeds and
scrap wood, small icicles
in his shag, ice
on his muzzle. He is like
a carved calf, dropped in the snow
as if in his very tracks,
his front feet bent
as though in mid-trot, his
flank emaciated, bony structure
looming. A sculpture of a
white calf, lying on its side
in the snow at the side
of the barn, among things
cast off and forgotten.

Around his neck the rope
halter still dangles, beaded
with ice. They stop
a few feet away, silent, and stand
gravely looking, framing the thought
'Is it real?'—Not 'Is it alive,'
for they know at once it is
not that. But is it real
and not a toy, is a thing still real
once dead, a calf like a
plaster calf, lying frozen
in the snow, cast off
in its perfect stillness,
laid aside even though
perfect, looking realer
than real, untouchable, utterly
other?

A Night Window

Looking at losing you;
it's far away,
like headlights
that haven't yet crested the hill,
just a weird glow
in the sky—

or it's very near,
something to get
excited about, like
glimpsing what turns out to be
my eyelash, brushing
the microscope lens—

Looking at it like
looking at my
own face the dark pane
gives back: at what it sees,
neither surprised
nor resigned.

The Trust

Once I dreamed that a dead friend
wrote me a letter from beyond, complete
with return address; when I awoke
the name of the street eluded me,
but I remembered the message, a
short one, only this,
he wanted to tell me:
"The work goes on."

And when my grandfather lay
in the hospital, settling his account
with cancer, he replied
to all who inquired of him, "I'm just
waiting for a visa," he would say.
"Tell them, I'm waiting for a visa."

And I remember
how he looked at me, two days
before the end—
looked and looked,
as if to store me up—
and held me with his eyes
intent in love; and then
how he closed them, saying
"I can still see you, I see you
with my eyes closed. I'll
remember you." Smiling.

A good death, it's a gift
to the living. To be remembered
when we're gone, to remember our dead, these
we know are to be desired. But to be
remembered by our dead! that
is something else—a trust,
a blessing.

Fatherhood hits a man

Fatherhood hits a man
like a bolt, like sunstroke.
It stuns him; he sees stars.
For months afterward
he shines, his smooth
forehead shines, his eyes
gleam above dark shadows
of broken sleep, his face
beams his new stature,
even his watchband glitters
more brightly on his hairy arm,
catches light
to catch the dim
gaze of the newborn.

The shining father: shines
like the watch he dangles
over the crib
to gurgles and waving arms—
the watch upon whose second-hand
he hung so recently, timing
contractions: it has already begun
to tick off the seconds
of this other life.

Alive

I saw a landing gull
haul in his wings
from flight, and thought:

'There is a going out into the dark
and a coming in out of the dark
one finds oneself between.

As between the ringing
of the hammer in cold air,
and the actual hammer-blow, witnessed
at a distance.

Or between the object and the
extremity of its lengthened
evening shadow.

Or between the words that come
out of the mouth, and those
that were in the mind before.'

One hovers
between the whole egg
and its breaking.

Labour: Tract for the Obstetrician

Consider the mother, the child,
as a single motion. As moving continually
in and out of each other.
It is not one who gives birth
to the other, but birth which is given
by each to the other, constantly,
in a single fluid movement.
There is a tunnel, but it is not the tunnel
inside the mother, for the mother
is herself inside of it, moving down it
at an awesome speed—and in this tunnel
there is no child. There is only breath.
And colour: as when the palms press
against shut eyelids—hot colour
that changes in waves, colour surging
and deepening, colour hanging
on the edge of breath, and proceeding
from breath. At the end of the tunnel,
a splash. Like the splash
of a fish that jumps in black water
before dawn, sending the first ripples
rushing across water, hungry for shore.
(But at the centre, nothing.)

The splash will surprise the whole body
as the eye is surprised by a star's falling.
Then—nothing. For seconds, the absolute nothing
which is all there is: it is the nothing
we all came from, the nothing we are here
to find our way back to. *Stand back from this.*

For seconds. (And then
the magnetizing cry...

Blackberries

Naomi with a full pail fell:
a tangle in the bramble looped
her ankle round, and caught it
like a hand, to pull her down
into the grassy gully, where she found
herself upon her back, the pail aloft
and upright, held secure against her chest.
Scarcely a berry spilled
of the precious catch! And so she lay
among the leaves, and laughed.

Bandana girl, gatherer,
ditch-leaper, rock-scrambler,
bringer of bounty, may you always
find plenty, and safely
come home.

Villanelle for a Cool April

I like a leafing-out by increments,
—not bolting bloom, in sudden heat begun.
Life's sweetest savoured in the present tense.

I like to watch the shadows pack their tents
before the creep of the advancing sun.
I like a leafing-out by increments:

to watch the tendrils inch along the fence,
to take my pleasures slow and one by one.
Life's sweetest savoured in the present tense.

Oh, leave tomorrow's fruit to providence
and dote upon the bud—from which is spun
a leafing-out to love in increments,

a greening in the cool of swooning sense,
a feathered touch, a button just undone.
Life's sweetest savoured in the present tense,

as love when it withholds and then relents,
as a cool April lets each moment stun.
I like a leafing-out by increments;
life's sweetest savoured in the present tense.

Stormblue

"You're rich, and you want to be loved like a poor man."
–*Les enfants du paradis*

The way a woman loves a man
without money: for the holes
in his socks, for the tilt
of his eyebrows, for his voice
singing a song or murmuring
behind a door, for the fragrant
smoke of his pipe bluing the air
in the small old cozy cluttered room,
for his patched elbows, his
tweedy jackets from the Nearly New,
for the blind intelligence
of his body in love, for his hands,
quiet on the table, their dance
in the air when he speaks,
for the mole
on the back of his neck, for a few
old jokes that he likes to tell,
for his laugh,
for the way his hair sticks up
in the morning, for the cleft
in his chin, for a dimple
(seldom seen) in his left cheek,
for his dreams, and the light
that they put in his eyes
evenings of dreamy talk —

For the blue of his eyes
that she calls
his baby eyes
that grow stormblue
in anger at being loved
for the foolish things
she loves him for,

because they are all he has
to give her,
because he knows
that she knows
he will never
have more.

Astronomy

In a borrowed country house
night after night, she falls asleep
alone, a lamp still burning.
Out on the deck, or in the field
behind the house, he scans the sky,
Handbook of the Heavens in his hand.
Star maps and star charts. Evening
after evening, after the dinner things
are put away, he studies these
in silence. Spreads them out
across the table, under the hanging light
in its basket shade (which gently swings,
and the light's circle swings
around him, coming to rest
in increments)
                            Her small cough,
far across the room, where she's sunk
deep in the mildewed chair with the sagging springs,
is barely heard.
                            It's so quiet,
she thinks, you could almost
call it peaceful. She turns a page.
She looks at him, and looks away.

So pass the August days.
Another year; they have
another year to sleepwalk through
before they're done,
before he's gone.

Only then
will she have questions
about the stars.

Station

The gulls around the space ship
in front of the science museum
seem to like the space ship.
They seem to be
thinking about it, too,
walking in circles on the polished grass
and casting it sidelong glances as the light
glances off their polished backs.

So much clean bright whiteness here
on the flat smooth green
at summer noon!
We come to a halt
before it—who would not?—and gaze.
The gulls are white as envelopes,
and circulate. The stationary
hull reverberates with gleam.

Not what we came to see—
two travellers, refugees
of our own pasts,
come for the day on business—
still, we have
(for no clear reason to be fathomed)
to pause here, hand in hand,
trying to net a thought,

blank as the gulls
and the mute ship poised for flight
it will not take. The thought
that beats, propeller-like,
above our heads
is that we're here—
wherever we were before,
wherever we mean to be.

Redoing the Entrance

Today the stairs end in mid-air, halfway down.
I see you at the bottom—pencil in hand,
chewing your lip, assessing with slight frown
the space you've opened for the curved stairs planned
in place of straight ones. —You've got it figured out,
you tell me—smell of hot sawdust on the air—
you see how you can do it. (Scenting my doubt?)
I gaze down at the sawdust in your hair,
and wonder at the faith that made the cut
before the plans were drawn. The way you are.
The way you made me yours—not asking what
could go wrong—trusting we'd come this far.
And how you've placed a table for a landing,
so I can climb down now, to where you're standing.

On Closing the Apartment
of My Grandparents of Blessed Memory

And then I stood for the last time in that room.
The key was in my hand. I held my ground,
and listened to the quiet that was like a sound,
and saw how the long sun of winter afternoon
fell slantwise on the floorboards, making bloom
the grain in the blond wood. (All that they owned
was once contained here.) At the window moaned
a splinter of wind. I would be going soon.

I would be going soon; but first I stood,
hearing the years turn in that emptied place
whose fullness echoed. Whose familiar smell,
of a tranquil life, lived simply, clung like a mood
or a long-loved melody there. A lingering grace.
Then I locked up, and rang the janitor's bell.

Into the Nineties

Thin is the veneer
of newness on this renovated house
built early in the century. The floors
are sanded to the quick.
They will not take
another sanding. Now that the
glossy finish, rolled on slick,
has flaked away in spots,
and winter dryness cracks the weaker boards
so that they catch the foot and splinter off,
we see: it is an old floor.
No help for it.

And in the night
the banging in the pipes,
and the slow seep
of dust, out from between
the mortared bricks
of one old wall laid bare
for elegance...

So snows the old,
spreading its sediment
on all our furnishings, a
fine grime.

The World Is Its Own Museum

What is this box of shapes
that I'm assembling?
It is not a question to ask.

Say I assemble a box of shapes
as every human does, because my eye,
lighting on them, likes them,
because "life" is an inversion of "file",
because the world is its own museum.

It is not a question to ask,
running one's finger over the
. dusty contours of the unidentified.

I assemble a box of shapes
as every human does,
watching them gather dust
in their corner—as we all
clutter our corners with the unidentified.
We are collectors all, and our
collections are collectors too,
collecting dust.

Still I assemble a box of shapes
because my eye, lighting on them,
likes them—as my eye (come fresh
from the dazzle of afternoon
into the gloomy entranceway) lights too
with pleasure upon the hall
table where one has placed
the bowl of what's currently blooming.

A Solstice Rose

I prop my drooping rose
(its toppled head
hung on the limp stalk
of its spent neck)

first, on a wishful finger:
tilting the vase this way
and that, for a point
of balance that won't endure;

then, on a twist-tie's wrapped
wire, fished from a drawer
to fashion a spiral collar.
There, my dear; linger;

I've bought you a day's grace.
Drink up, stand tall. Trap
in the shady overlap
of your milky petals, some pale

December sun (its pearl
like yours, ephemeral)
as I've trapped your nodding head
awake, in a brace of metal.

Rattled

Something has jarred loose in the mind.
An old grief, like a marble rolling around
in an empty drawer—hitting the sides
and rolling again, making a hollow
wavering aimless scrawl of sound.

A winter fly, trapped between windowpanes,
wakens to buzz the dusty glass.

The heart has its stops and starts.
Sometimes you wake with the taste
of death in your mouth,
like bitter silver.

Moments on a Balcony

He says, 'These birds
sometimes fill the air like confetti,
a handful of confetti, tossed up
or tossed down.'

And her eye too has tracked
their flocking, but her head
is elsewhere utterly,
with the uncles on Arlington,
and the scuttlebutt from Nantucket.

They sit in a swoon of linden.
It is the midpoint
of the year's midsummer light.
They yawn beneath the awning.

She says, 'Oh, but I liked
the backlit lambs, their haloes.'
She remembers a dream then,
a dream of running for cover.

It darkens above her
like an approaching storm.
She thinks, *We are not young any more.*

The birds twist up again
like a scarf of black chiffon.

Ponte Vedra

It was lizard hour in the lanai.
The lizards were running back and forth
on the white ceramic tiles, under the white
wrought iron chairs. The smell of the earth
rose evening-deep from the corner beds.
It was a Roman hour
of twilit clarity: air
like white wine, the palm fronds
darkening in sky's apricot afterglow,
white villas across the lagoon
revealing as in a dream the mathematical
purity of their lines and spacing.

It was an hour free of sediment
or sentiment. Pure as a baby's yawn.
Without price. A thing in itself,
like a marble egg, reflecting
things-in-themselves. It did not
want for anything. It was not
to be bought or sold, and nothing
needed to be bought on its account.
In it nothing was quite real, but things
were as they seemed. A languid hour
in the lanai on the lagoon.
Florida, redeemed.

Riveted

It is possible that things will not get better
than they are now, or have been known to be.
It is possible that we are past the middle now.
It is possible that we have crossed the great water
without knowing it, and stand now on the other side.
Yes: I think that we have crossed it. Now
we are being given tickets, and they are not
tickets to the show we had been thinking of,
but to a different show, clearly inferior.

Check again: it is our own name on the envelope.
The tickets are to that other show.

It is possible that we will walk out of the darkened hall
without waiting for the last act: people do.
Some people do. But it is probable
that we will stay seated in our narrow seats
all through the tedious dénouement
to the unsurprising end—riveted, as it were;
spellbound by our own imperfect lives
because they are lives,
and because they are ours.

A Confused Heart

All right, I admit it, I'm to blame,
it's on account of me
the Messiah doesn't come;

I am the blip on the screen,
the cold spot, the dark area you see
with indefinite borders, moving sluggishly

crabwise, with a density all its own,
unabsorbed, indissoluble; the clot
in the body politic—that's me,

accountable by myself (though not alone)
for the tarrying footfall, for our
continuing bad name:

because of my imperfect faith,
my ritual omissions, my mistakes in form,
my little games of nor-care-I,

because I am stiff-necked, and push
the quarrel with God one step too far,
preferring to do the thing my way

rather than not at all (unable
to play by the rules to save my life,
unwilling to drop the ball)—

because I confuse having a part
with holding apart, and star with shield;
because I will always pause

in my studies along the road, to say
How fair is that field,
how fine is that tree;

because I have made strange fire
again and again, and lived,
and the earth has not swallowed me.

Circa 2000

Imperatives of Get and Spend
still ruled the day.

The sunlight was different.
It had been whitening
over a decade, year by year.
No one talked of this.

The ubiquitous young
of the city, shorn and pierced,
cluttered the bases of the monuments.
In your face, they said. *In your dreams.*

There was the small racket of a
toybox being dumped
or combed—this was the
foreground noise. Behind it,
distant sirens.

People were having a
fulsome interlude with a
lady poet, but they still
watched tv.
Some booed the anthem.
There were blessings
circulating privately.

Wireborne viruses took
the spotlight. Meanwhile, as wreckers
arrived to gut the derelict sanatorium,
.White Plague was making a
quiet comeback.

Superstition was collecting
like a brown mist in ditches
by the side of the road.
Jerusalem was up for grabs again.

Some of us had our ear
to the wall. We were a
mind willing to change.

The Unharmed

War has a long wake. Waves of two long wars
washed us up slapped and gasping, upside down,
into our here and now:
their storm-swell, slow subsiding,
our cradle rocking.   What could we know
of what it smashed before?
Cushioned upon its gentled lap and slap
we doze awake, ride high and dry
the caulked cocoons of our unearned lives.

We are the generation spared,
bubbles of a rolling boil
whose heat we never felt,
coddled and cosseted and silver-spooned,
unmindful of our luck—to have been dealt
so charmed a hand, in an unforgiving world!
—So we stand, the unharmed,
mute by the cenotaph,
reading the names of some who died.

We are the message in the bottle
bobbing unopened on the ebbing tide:
a cipher on a slip
of paper curled
around the Reason Why.
We are the writing that stayed dry,
and cannot read itself.

Levels

In this city the hospitals
are on the hill, the sick look down
from their high place, upon the tortuous
peregrinations of the well,
or they look up, they gaze on the serene
procession of clouds. And theirs
is the realm between.

I think of you up there,
remote behind your allocated pane,
your porthole on the man-swarm
and eternity. No way to know
which way you're facing now,
what side you'll exit on, this time,
how much you think on it, or care.

A life is a life. What
will we make of that?
What is the real world?
Privately, no one believes
he's living in it.

We are about to begin the descent,
the voice says. We say: *I've paid my dues.*

Sunset. It is the hour when hospital windows
beam gold into the eyes
of runners on the upper avenues.

Day Visit

He had already turned to walk away
When she looked back. And he did not look back.
The train began to inch along the track,
Then picked up speed, then left the station bay.
She stowed her knapsack on the luggage rack.
Through banks of cloud, one broad bedazzling ray
Of setting sun shone red on bales of hay
In autumn fields. She watched the land go black.

She thought she understood him: why prolong
A valediction in the afternoon—
A visit preordained to end too soon?
(She'd made the reservation to be strong.)
Why *should* he pause to wave? Proper goodbyes
Are crisp. Besides, the sun was in his eyes.

To N, *in absentia*

I do not know how you went out of my life
or when exactly. The leaves of the Norway maple
are beginning to turn yellow, fall has come.
I last saw you on an evening at the end of July
but I think you were already gone then,
I think by then you had been gone for a long time.

And so it seems meaningless to count the days
yet still I count them, August, September,
October now half over, terrible days,
and I do not know where you are
or when I may have news of you again.
But I remember as if yesterday the day
you came out of my body into this world,
a fine splash in full midsummer, a small cry
like the meow of a Siamese cat,
your eyes wide open and looking all around;
remember how in the early hours of that morning,
before you arrived, I heard pass down our street
(as I had heard each morning of that summer
of my thirtieth year) the clopping sound
of a lone horse pulling a calèche,
his sleepy driver bound for the road
that climbs Mount Royal's slope.

No one can take away that morning
or the exactness of its place in time.
I go there often.
I visit it like a temple.

Bounty

Make much of something small.
The pouring-out of tea,
a drying flower's shadow on the wall
from last week's sad bouquet.
A fact: it isn't summer any more.

Say that December sun
is pitiless, but crystalline
and strikes like a bell.
Say it plays colours like a glockenspiel.
It shows the dust as well,

the elemental sediment
your broom has missed,
and lights each grain of sugar spilled
upon the tabletop, beside
pistachio shells, peel of a clementine.

Slippers and morning papers on the floor,
and wafts of iron heat from rumbling rads,
can this be all? No, look—here comes the cat,
with one ear inside out.
Make much of something small.

The Orchestre du Conservatoire Rehearses
in Salle St-Sulpice

Come with me now: round to the side entrance
and down the marble stairs,
past the Sunday dwarf who guards the *Vestiaire*,
to the basement hall with its faint smell
of a scooped-out pumpkin—quickly, come,

we are late, you see—already
the bows are sliding up and down
under the dim spotlights where smoke
from morning cigarettes collects to hang
like a blue island on the musty air...

You can write your name in dust
on the wooden seats of the fold-down chairs
where the hinged cases lie open
like empty carapaces, lined in old plush
motheaten blue or threadbare red

blackened by tarnish from silver keys
or dandruffed by rosin. On the *scène*
the *chef d'orchestre*, haloed by wild hair,
bohemian in a new red flannel shirt
points at the brass with trembling stick,

and the bell of a French horn, raised on cue,
gleams a reply. One long golden note
hurts into being, drawn out pure till he
clips it off with a flick—then drops into a
mincing squat, hissing

Pianissimo!
(and beyond the heavy drapes, out
on the snowy street, making moan,
the hooded pigeons promenade
to a solemn bonging of bells.)

Getting In Deeper

You were about to read from your
new collection of poems, entitled *Four
Deepsea Dives of the English Language*, when
someone in the front row stood up and
accused you in front of everyone! It was
a fairly serious charge, too: *You knew
about the body in the basement.*
Well. There was only one thing to do.

Holding your head high you quietly
walked off the stage, straight out the
side exit and down the hall until
you saw a room marked 'Ladies', where you knew
you could discreetly disburden yourself
of your large wad of Bazooka gum.
This took care of your main worry. Some
college girls seemed to be watching, though.

It wasn't the time to linger and admire
the naked babies rolling like porpoises
in the row of aquariums that were really
toilet-tanks. This was just as well,
because you realized all at once that your
train would be leaving in ten minutes!
You ran like hell and just made it. What a relief.
Only it seemed you had forgotten your Chinese flute...

The High Meadows

As the afternoon shadows of hills
move across each other's faces
so do the decades cast shadows:
deep shadows have flooded whole folds
of the time that's left me,
extinguishing the light once cupped
in their embrace, each space
its own measure of warm gold
doused now, put to sleep,
smoking green-blue, blue-
black, a whisper
of haze and fade.
How few are the places left
that the sun has not abandoned!
the high meadows! I will run
to gain them while the light lasts,
run and run uphill,
a late sprint
with night's cool breath
at my shoulder.

As a storm-lopped tree

As a storm-lopped tree corrects its shape
over a few green seasons, so time
closes around the hole in itself
left by the terrible event.

(in the quiet room suddenly the ice
in your glass hisses and cracks—)

So years have carried you, far beyond
the site of your old derailment,
the place where once you caused
harm to yourself and others;
it is behind you now,
and the damage, behind us all.

The chain belt of time
runs around and around.
Moon walks where it wants to,
like cats in high places.
Sun gilds the buildings...

And moments of animal well-being
may be all that's left us, may well be.

To be grateful for neutral days.

To snip a strip of char
from a blackened wick, then watch
how the lamp comes alive again.

A Prayer for Prayer

God! I am dead empty.
Pour me full again.
I am leaden; lighten me.
My cables are cut.

Pour me full again,
a freshly brimming cup.
My cables are cut.
Oh, hook me up!

A freshly brimming cup,
sunstruck, flashing sun's fire:
oh, hook me up,
string me like a lyre

sunstruck, flashing sun's fire,
by this wintry window.
String me like a lyre
and let the hours pluck,

by this wintry window,
a tune from taut gut.
Oh, let the hours pluck
a psalm: forsake me not!

A tune from taut gut:
I am leaden; lighten me.
A psalm: *Forsake me not,*
God! I am dead empty.

Gate

A pause to pull socks up.

It seems the time has come
to check your raggedy sadnesses
at the gate,
and take your place in line again
for the roulette of days.

Time to turn your back on
that other one, your nemesis,
a face that looks backward and weeps
while the feet walk blind
into the future;
time to drop hands with that one.

You have come into a place
of unbleached reckoning.
It is like
an empty dress,
wind filling an empty dress
hung out to air,
revolving slowly on its hanger,
catching the sun in its full
sleeves, in its folds and weave.

Hope, that shy fern,
has begun to unfurl its plume
from the rotted stump of your
cut down dream.

Echoes in November

Correspondences are everywhere,
things that shadow things,
that breathe or borrow
essence not their own;
and so the yellow leaves
that, singly, streak
in silence past a black
uncurtained pane
(catching the lamplight from within
as they dart down)
have the elusiveness
of shooting stars,
and so it sometimes happens
that you pause
in kitchen ministrations,
knife in hand
above the chopping board,
savouring, raw, a stub
of vegetable not destined
for the pot,
and faintly tasting
at the back of the palate
the ghost of a rose
in the core of the carrot.

Run With It

The road through the park
is littered with sticks
discarded by dogs
on their morning walks.
Sticks don't go home with dogs.
Dropped by the wayside
they lie in wait,
like the theories of philosophers.

Messenger

Little stone in my shoe,
what have you to tell me?
That such a tiny irritant can serve
to undermine a meditative mood
hard-won from day's commotion
by a walker on the mountain?
That I am obstinate, who will not stoop,
or stop to teeter on one leg
and tug at sandal-straps—
prefer to hope you'll work your way
out, same way you sidled in,
without my intervention?

Are you a stowaway—fugitive,
or just adventurer
hopping a ride to town,
a roadside pebble with big-city dreams?
Are you a terrorist—dispatched
to tell the plight of kindred
tired of being trodden on?
Are you a grain of sand,
seed for a pearl to my oyster brain?
Are you an augurer?

You cling and dig in
even to toughened skin,
and will not be appeased.
Little stone in my shoe,
what makes me choose
to walk with you awhile?
What little creeping guilt
accepts it as my lot
that you should harry my sole
the whole way home?

Lowly

Pink as discarded chewing gum
it comes to the surface in rain.
Segmented like a bellows.
Hoisting its length in sections
along puddled asphalt.
It is all muscle; elastic.
It draws itself forward in rhythms
of flex and slack.
It retracts when touched.

It is mute.
It abides in the dark, under porches.
It operates below ground
its tunnelings aerate.
It thrives on decay—
each day
casts many times its weight
in black gold,
giving back better than it takes.
It is the sign of living earth.

Hand picked, dropped in a tin can,
it is the fisherman's best friend.
It dwells in the smell
of good black loam
and the moisture thereof.
And it is moist, and gleams
in the loam like a tongue.

When caught, it writhes.
When cold, it goes deeper
underground and weaves itself
into a ball of its kind.
Slice it with a spade

and it seems
at least one part
survives,
burrowing back
into churned dirt.
Intact, it will die
when dry.
It shuns the sun.

Poem on Father's Day

There appears suddenly, out of nowhere,
a blemish in the mirror
on a piece of sentimental furniture,
a bubble in the bevel
of the scalloped border.

Where are you now, my father,
fifty-four years gone,
whose adolescent face once looked
back at itself from this mirror?
(Father it wasn't given me to know.
Father I never called on Father's Day.)

Truth burns through a dream.
Sometimes I have felt
your presence in a dream,
have dreamed about you.
Today, thinking of you,
I dialed your brother, last
of the living uncles.

But how am I to read
this pucker in the silver?
A flaw, shaped like a tear.
Last time I looked, it wasn't there.

It is your mother's face
that looks back at me now
from the glass—she who outlived you
forty-eight years—but not the wizened face
I said goodbye to; it is her face
as you last knew it, face I remember
from when I was small,
I see framed here.

The son I named for you
turns thirty this week.

Somewhere at the back of my mind
an old clock goes on chiming the quarters,
a clock of my childhood.

Parents

It is in the nature
of a mother
to hover.
All mothering
is at least one part
hovering.
What would you rather?
Angels in heaven
also hover—sometimes fall.
We all have the mothers
we were given. And
breakable fathers.

Are you serious?

What is that little grating chink
in college girls' voices, like the chirp
of glass marbles rubbed together
in a child's palm?
It is some kind of hope
they are grinding in their throats,
a virus they catch from one another.
It is like birds that cock their heads
at the foot of picnic tables.
They think it will fetch them something.

Flash

The heat of the immediate:
where is it now?
Was it our portion only for a spell,
like children's breath on windowpanes
in which to trace the day's
faces and names?
Damp breath exhaled on glass,
a cloud on which to skate
a stuttering finger—
quick, while it lasts—

Heat was a given, we thought.
Heat of connection.
Heat of breeding.
Our hot palms on the world.
Then a coolness set in.
When did it begin?

Heat of the immediate
is leaving me now,
surging up through the stem of me
in periodic gusts,
making me its conduit
to the world outside.
I who was warm in the world
and warmed by it
now do my part in warming it,
delivering my small
caloric quota to air's waiting arms,
in calibrated increments
that cool me as they go.

Cooled will I abide
in the world then,
till breath no longer clouds the mirror—

till one day, also briefly, my decay
will warm an inch or two
of the encompassing clay.

Blowing the Fluff Away

for E. B.

The sprig of unknown bloom you sent last fall
spent the long winter drying on my wall,
mounted on black. But it had turned to fluff
some months ago. Tonight I took it down
because I thought that I had had enough
of staring at it. Brittle, dry and brown,
it seemed to speak too plainly of a waste
of friendship, forced to flower, culled in haste.

So, after months of fearing to walk past
in case the stir should scatter it to bits,
I took it out to scatter it at last
with my own breath, and so to call us quits.
—Fooled! for the fluff was nothing but a sheath,
with tiny, perfect flowers underneath.

Brush

Always a wild openness
to the left and right of our path,
a humming in the high grasses.
What is it holds us to our course?

A pagan recklessness in my past
makes me conservative.

Today when I was reading on the balcony
a bee buzzed my knuckle, close enough
for me to feel the wind of his wings,

and all day long I have gone on feeling
the wind of those wings.

Cameo

Remembering our younger selves
in the rain.
Ducking under stairways, sheltering.
Streetlamps reflected trembling
in cold puddles.
It was February or early March,
an early thaw, not yet spring,
it must have been soon after we met;
we were barely acquainted then,
nothing had begun for us yet.
What were we doing there
on Lorne Avenue, that night,
in the rain? Heads together,
whispering. Where had we been?
Going home to separate rooms,
but taking our time.
We were students;
it seems to me now
we were children still.
The smell was of spring.
Rainsound a thin pecking
at the last snow crusts.
Rain dripping from the landings.
We were hushed, listening.
We could not know
the brink we stood on.

My Shoes Are Killing Me
(a poem in nine movements)

i   You Could Almost Understand

It was the beginning of dwindle.
Even the ink was stingy.
The doctor was mortal.

Some of the stickiness had worn off
the things we had to do.
For a while they still clung, like bits
of wet Scotch tape. Some washed away
in rains that came. We let them go.

Rain was falling through my
burnt gazebo.

One morning I thought I saw the last
unevaporated dewdrop in the grass,
among the little shaggy heads of white clover
(second-growth, end-of-summer clover)
and I said *Where is my trampoline?*
I said *Where is my toboggan?*
Where are my monkey bars, I said,
and *Where is my roller-skate key?*
Where is my brain, was the real question.
It seemed to have wandered off.

Then the lights went down and suddenly
it was a movie about trees, no, not *about*,
it was a movie of trees,
it was a movie of trees moving
in wind, and of branches heaving
in wind, and the sound
was of wind soughing in branches

and of great rushes of wind in leaves
(the sound dying down then starting up again
at some other spot in the wall of greenery)
and there was no other sound
but the layers of whoosh and wind-rush
in the lashing wall of greenery,
no other sound but what the trees
were saying to each other in the wind
in their own language,
and there were no subtitles,
but you could almost understand
what the trees were saying.

ii   A Yellowing

It was the beginning of dwindle.

I was imagining a museum
of dead sounds, a repository
for the lost soundtrack
of daily life, horse-clop on city streets,
tinkle of winter sleighbells, thunder of coal
down coal-chutes, the peck and clack
of manual typewriters (*zing*
of their carriages and *ting*
of their carriage-bells),
clock-tick and clock-chime,
the milkman's jangling carry-crates,
noon whistles, squeak of clothesline pulleys,
"Chopsticks" on parlour pianos,
five o'clock carillon tunes
and radio jingles advertising
products long gone from shelves near you,
You'll wonder where the yellow went
when you brush your teeth with Pepsodent,

(only you won't any more,
you will not wonder, for
the yellow is ever with us,
yellow the colour of dwindle
and dwindle a yellowing
of pages, kitchen ceilings, bathroom tiles,
net curtains and Venetian blinds,
and Indian cottons stowed in trunks,
and Kodachrome in albums,
thinning skin in elbow creases,
thickening footsole calluses,
our jaundiced hopes
like flat champagne
in last night's unwashed glasses)

And I said *Where is my trampoline?*
I said *Where is my toboggan?*
Where are my monkey bars, I said.

And I wanted to write subtitles
for a movie of trees rustling in wind.

iii   Dominion Observatory Time Signal

> *"The beginning of the long dash following ten seconds of silence*
> *marks exactly one o'clock, Eastern Standard Time."*

Beep. Beep. Beep. Beep. Beep. Beep.   *Beeeeeeeeeep.*

This is a sound I used to hear
on the kitchen radios of my childhood,
over the churn of the Thor washing machine
and lunch-hour smells of Campbell's Soup.
I was going to give it pride of place
in my Museum of Lost Sounds,
but it turns out this is not a lost sound,

this is *Canada's longest-running but shortest radio program*,
first broadcast on November 5, 1939,
and you can still hear it on the radio every day
(*"very little changed"*, though I haven't tried)
if you tune in to the right station
at the right time.
                              —So I have learned,
and was amazed to learn,
but I haven't tried.

This is not a lost sound.
But the child who heard it back then
is a lost child,
and I prefer to leave it undisturbed
in her ears

The Dominion Observatory Time Signal

The beginning of the long dash
for that child

iv   Something Was Missing

It was the beginning of dwindle.
No one was in the castle.
Summer was slipping away like a small
snake into a crack between rocks,
too quickly to grasp its bright pattern,
a rustle, a movement
in the corner of the eye
of something dappled and sinuous, fleeting,
cornucopia of smells wafting in
through the summer screen door,
and something was missing now
from what used to be enough,

when did we first notice
it wasn't enough?

A decade now goes by like water.
Kiss it goodbye.

I could get all the way across my monkey bars.
I didn't have to let go half way
and drop to the ground, stirring up
ignominious dust. (After, I'd flex
stiff hands, palms stained with rust.)
And I could jump from the top step,
describing an arc in the air to clear
the bottom stoop
                    and land smack
on the front walk (hands to cement
to break momentum)
bearing the shock and sting
of impact in my soles.

Like a doctor's slap
on the day we first draw breath—

Summer was slipping away,
and the river had begun to run backward.
And I said *Where is my trampoline?*
I said *Where is my toboggan?*
And a little herd of dry leaves
came drifting across my path.
The wind was their shepherd.

v Mixed Drink

A little herd of dry leaves.
They shall not want.
They shall crumble into soil and become
food for next year's greening,
food for green pastures

and the river has begun to run backward,
has begun to run
forwards and backwards,
like an estuary at its widening,
a salt wedge driving inland towards childhood
while freshets of Now press seaward,
a mixing of waters, salt and sweet

(my toboggan got away from me,
went kiting down the slope uncaptained,
light as a paper boat, bumping and bouncing
while I watched from the crest of the hill)

Fill the dark jug of Change
from the river that runs both ways,
and pour our cup.
This is the water we shall drink
for the rest of our days,
salt and sweet,

but we're still in the game, still waiting
to hear our numbers called, our cards are
half filled, we're sticking it out
all the way to Bingo.

vi Each Day Running Out

> *One, two.*
> *Buckle my shoe.*

I remember the bronzed baby shoes
atop television sets, next to the
baby portraits in silver frames.
What were they all about?
First of the outgrown shoes.
Like cast-off shells
of the soft pink animal foot.

Auntie Sylvia, back from synagogue,
sank into her favourite chair,
eased her feet out of her pinching Sabbath shoes,
and sighed her last words: *Ahhh… it's good*
to come home. Her heart gave out right there.
The legendary end of Auntie S.,
her memory be blessed. Her card
half filled. Envy her her exit.

Undo your shoes,
before they undo you.

It was the beginning of dwindle, it was the end
of summer endlessness. Something was missing
from what used to be enough,
the cup of summer running over,
summer's full cup. Each day running
out into the bird-loud morning
before sun toppled the blocks of shade,
a barefoot dash across soaking grass
to tilt dew off the seats of the swings—

And later: flat dull metal disc
of my roller-skate key. Fitting the sockets
round those blunt square bolts, turning it
tighter and tighter, till it wouldn't turn,
till the skate's metal pincers gripped
both sides of a scuffed shoe
and gave it wings—

vii   Time Capsule

And for a while we flew.

(rhythmic click of sidewalk cracks,
and giddy clicklessness
on blacktop, velvet bands of new-rolled tar—
then to unstrap, and walk on air
the height of phantom wheels,
and feel the phantom tingle in our soles
deep into peachy afternoon)

   each day running out

Now it's pedestrian plod, in shoes that rub.
Ay, there's the rub: the chafe
of the quotidian. How many times
can a person make dinner? wash up the dishes?
cut one's fingernails? it is all,
and always, to do again,

while things we didn't do, and never will,
queue up on the wires like birds
and wing off, one by one,

or we remove them from our sleeve
(the sleeve we wore them on, next to our hearts),

retire them to a little box
to bury in the garden (but, what garden?
the garden's also buried in the box—)

And our old doctor's dead.

This is the vestibule where we change
our shoes for paper slippers.
This is the waiting room.
Beyond that door
is the cold table where you lie
under the tracking of a radiant eye,
attended by angels in lead aprons.
Take a number.

viii   Ravelled Sleeve

I wanted to write subtitles
for a movie of trees rustling in wind,
for I have always loved the sound
of wind in leaves, the sound of trees
talking to each other in their own language,
and I have always known
that what they say is true.

What did I dream?
Thudding—there was something to do with
thudding but I don't remember
what. Something was thudding.
Something maybe to do with
time?
        it wasn't my heart

        Something was racing—

(In the hospital on the hill
meds are dispensed with dinner
in little fluted cups.)

It was the beginning of dwindle, it was the end
of sleeve-repairing sleep—the start
of a ravelled wakefulness, of lying
with eyes wide open in the dark.
Sudden gusting in a midnight alley.
A clangor of empty trash cans
knocked over and rolling. And a
banging of loose doors in the wind —

> *A box is buried in the garden,*
> *and in that box, a garden's buried,*
> *garden we planned but never planted,*
> *dream of a garden,*
> *sealed in a box of dreams.*

ix   Enough

It was the beginning of dwindle.
Sons towered over us.
Daughters, calling long distance,
asked hard questions.
A blight was upon the maples,
spotting the leaves with tar,
and moths were back.

Rain was falling through the
rusty monkey bars
in empty city playgrounds.

It was the beginning of knowing
we were running out of days.

Something was thudding.
Something was racing.
And the ink was stingy—
late nights so quiet I could hear my
pen scratching paper. Penscratch.
Henscratch. Where's the egg?

End-of-summer windows still open
to let in the night air,
and sometimes I thought I could hear
a different wind stirring the trees,
and sometimes I thought one could learn
to find Enough again,
to let what-used-to-be-enough
(summer's cup running out)
be enough—given a few more years.

The truth of it:
summers were never any longer
than they are now.

I sat down on the wooden bench
and undid my shoes.

And I said *Where is my trampoline?*

Castoffs

Poignancy of the discarded.
The armless doll that stares
from the trash heap in spring,
the sagging sofa with the cat-scratched arms,
the love-stained mattress in the rain.
Inside-out umbrellas, broken-ribbed,
flapping forlornly in puddles,
and jack-o-lanterns after Hallowe'en,
askew on compost piles.

Poignancy even of the intact, discarded:
here, today, curbside by the corner post
(among junked chairs and rust-stained mops)
a perfectly good birdcage
with all the fittings: porcelain cups
for seed and water,
ladders, mirrors—all the bells
and whistles—everything
but the bird.

Gleanings at Year's End

At a New Year's party
you learn to count to ten
in Mandarin: *yi, ar, sun, sseh, woo,*
liu, chi, ba, jeow, sheu.
It remains to be seen what good
this will ever do you. Earlier in the day,
the hostess sent an email
to apologize for cutting you off
on the phone: *I had a dog in my arms*
as I sat behind the steering wheel,
and you thought this could be
a metaphor for your life,
though you yourself have no dog,
and don't drive.

Seed

And the seed-bunches hung in the summer trees
on branches that swung in the wind,
it was the summer when everywhere you went
you heard the cries of newborn babies
out of open windows, or from behind fences
around private gardens, everywhere you went
there was a mother on the other
side of the wall

And the seed-bunches tossed in the wind
and you remembered the catalpas, their blooms
like spilled popcorn in the grass,
you remembered a dizzy old dress,
some silliness with a mattress on a roof
(no jumping back from memory
on its coiled spring,
jumping-jack memory
that says *Boo!*)
you remembered the chestnut that sprouted
in the children's sandbox one spring,
the sapling you nurtured in a flowerpot,
then in a bucket, then in a dug bed
where it grew to a sapling, then to a full-sized tree
that blossoms now each year
in front of a house no longer yours

And the seed-bunches tossed in the wind
on branches that swung and heaved,
it was the summer that came in the wake
of a birdless winter, first of the birdless winters,
it was the summer when everywhere you went
you heard the cries of newborns, and you felt
how all had changed, how all was changing,

summer of darkening horizons,
morrows gone treacherous,
a world dividing quickly
into King of the Castle
and Dirty Rascal

And you called out in your heart,
for the first time, to one on the way.
Impending, unexpected, cloud-bound child,
you are barreling towards me.

What We Keep

The last leaves came down in a warm wind
that blew all day on the fourteenth of November.
There were three balmy days in a row—we walked
in the park in the last sun of afternoon. Only the willows
still clung to their foliage, golden weeping willows,
sun catchers. We climbed a small hill. One of us
was in labour.

Do we all cling to grandeur of the past?
The ruins of the Parthenon loom over modern Greece,
and the laws of Temple sacrifice endure
in the synagogue prayer service.

Today a man in his fifties
showed me his first-grade workbook,
and a story he wrote on the reverse side
of a cereal box panel at the age of six,
and his first pair of baby shoes, saved
by the mother who abandoned him as a child;
these things sent to him in a box, decades later.
Proof that he once had a mother who loved him.

Segovia

The guitarists were sitting around
in somebody's basement room
discussing their fingernails.
They were comparing the length
of their fingernails, they were expounding
upon the strength of fingernails,
they were trading chilling tales
of broken fingernails.
The guitarists were filing the ragged
ends of their fingernails grown long
on one hand only, telltale sign,
badge of belonging to the cult,
and they could not afford tickets
to the Julian Bream concert
and they could not afford guitar lessons
but they had all the records,
they had the music, lovingly transcribed
off records, all by ear, hand-scratched
in India ink on music copy-sheets,
note by painstaking note. They had
the apocrypha, the word-of-mouth,
the heroes. Segovia was self-taught.

Breach

Always a surge of dark exultation
at the change of a season, a sparking
of memories. Today's:
a dawn walk in the city, sunless dawn
near the end of August, when you stepped
through a breach in a construction fence
to cut across an open lot—a sort of ruin,
rubble-strewn, between standing walls,
down near Chinatown. Smell of the river.
Not a soul in sight. No hint of a break
in the cloud cover—lowering sky,
the breeze damp, even clammy.
You were nineteen.
You weren't alone that day, but you were
alone. The hand you held
was noncommittal, loose in yours,
but it held. Nor did you drop it.
At the same time you hugged to yourself
some kind of inner blissful hard pure
aloneness that felt like treasure. A sense
of having embarked on open waters
in the frailest of crafts.
It could at any moment pour rain
on your bare arms— .
You mistook this for happiness.

Too Late

The power was out when we went to bed
that night, remember? It had been out
since suppertime—one of those late
afternoon thunderstorms
that used to roll through the valley
like a tidal wave. We blew out the candles,
forgetting which lights had been on,
forgetting about the radio
till, soon after we'd drifted off,
it jumped to life, full volume,
(along with the bedside lamp)
for a brutal second—just long enough
to jolt us awake with a dire,
frenetic male voice proclaiming, *"Too late!"*
For an instant we blinked at each other,
stupefied. You lunged for the radio knob
as the room went black again,
and there we lay, in country dark
(so much darker than city dark)
with that voice still echoing in our heads.
Was it too late? For what?
There were numerous possibilities.
Even back then, there were numerous
possibilities. The kids slept on, oblivious,
in their little rooms, their wooden bunks
under the flyspecked windows,
and after a moment we began to laugh,
a laugh we can reignite
with those words to this day.
Too late!
We dissolved in each other's arms
in helpless laughter.

Villanelle on a line from William Carlos Williams

So close are we to ruin every day!
A friend has lost her son; another's ill.
And *There but for the grace of God*, we say.

Some throw themselves into their work; some pray.
Some live as though there's no tomorrow. Still,
so close are we to ruin every day,

we know we only hold the dark at bay.
It peers at us beneath the curtain frill.
There but for the grace of God, we say.

Music hath charms. And wine. Salves that allay
night terrors—but we waken, and a chill
attends our brush with ruin another day:

whispers of trouble, come our neighbours' way.
How long before we taste the bitter pill
ourselves? *But for the grace of God*, we say,

and *Let us love each other, come what may.*
Brave words, half understood. Until, until.
We skirt the edge of ruin every day,
spared by the grace of God. Or so we say.

Please Have a Seat

You sit. And the vinyl
chair cushion slowly exhales.
Around you, banter
of strangers—the acid
camaraderie of the office.
Hard bright voices of women
around the coffee machine.
This is their domain.
Here they enact their days
that are not yours.

Who is behind the inner door?
Who, ensconced
on a high-backed leather throne,
will hear your sad petition?
He is The Appointed.
You have the appointment.
He has what you need,
but he is needy too.
Think of him as human while you wait.

So it goes in this world.
Think of him as needing.
Give him a face while you bide your time
there, in your chair,
clutching your requisition and the fee.
And burnish your words,

burnish the words
you'll tender as your plea.

An Infrequent Flyer Looks Down

The backwater of an airport lounge.
Across from us, overweight Americans
are eating ugly sandwiches.

Later I watch the ground recede.
Soon we are so high you can't
see a car unless it twinkles.

All my certainties, if I ever had any,
are out the window now.
Did I ever have any, or did I just
think I did? *All perception is gamble.*

Not a bead of thought today,
nothing but doubt.

What is worth wanting?
Consider the subversive hopefulness
of people who are starting over,
people who have lost everything.
The bankrupt optimism of an immigrant.

Give me a talisman, a charm to keep.
Give me a pebble for my pocket,
something to palm in secret.

Twinkle, twinkle, little car
way down there
running on your invisible
ribbon of road,
what are you running on?

Acknowledgements

Thank you first of all to Dan Wells of Biblioasis, for thinking to publish such a substantial retrospective of my poetry. I am grateful to Marc Plourde, Jack Hannan, and Bruce Taylor for generous time and thought given to helping me make this selection.

Thank you to the publishers of my previous collections represented here, beginning with the latest: Biblioasis, The Porcupine's Quill, Brick Books, House of Anansi Press, Cormorant Books, and Véhicule Press. Thank you to Fred Louder for beautiful design and printing of the chapbooks *The Space Between Sleep and Waking* (1981) and *Three Sestinas* (1984), back in our Villeneuve Publications days. And a nod to the late Fred Cogswell, who published my first title with Fiddlehead Poetry Books in 1978.

Acknowledgements are due the various publications (mainly literary magazines, some discontinued) where so many of these poems made their first appearances in print: *The American Voice*, *The Antigonish Review*, *Arc Poetry Magazine*, *Aurora: New Canadian Writing 1980*, *Books in Canada*, *The Canadian Forum*, *Canadian Notes & Queries*, *Canadian Poetry Now*, *The Fiddlehead*, *Jewish Quarterly*, *Literary Review of Canada*, *The Malahat Review*, *Matrix*, *The New Quarterly*, *North American Review*, *Nth Position*, *Ploughshares*, *Poetry* (Chicago), *Poetry Canada Review*, *Prairie Fire*, *Prism International*, *Rubicon*, *Scrivener*, *Shenandoah*, the *Times Literary Supplement*, *The Threepenny Review*, *Versus*, *The Walrus*, *West Coast Review*.

I would like to take this opportunity to thank Garrison Keillor of Minnesota Public Radio for bringing me many new readers with his broadcasts of my poems on The Writer's Almanac between 2005 and 2015.

Finally, I wish once again to thank the Canada Council for the Arts and the Conseil des arts et des lettres du Québec for grants that allowed me to begin or complete many of the poetry collections represented here.

About the Author

A poet, writer, literary editor, and musician, Robyn Sarah has lived in Montreal since early childhood. Her writing began to appear in Canadian literary magazines in the 1970s while she completed studies at McGill University and the Conservatoire de musique du Québec. She is the author of ten poetry collections, most recently *My Shoes Are Killing Me*, winner of the 2015 Governor General's Award for poetry and the Canadian Jewish Literary Award for poetry. She has also published two collections of short stories and a book of essays on poetry. Her poems have been published and anthologized in Canada, the US, and the UK, and since 2011 she has served as poetry editor for Cormorant Books.